An Easter Celebration

TRADITIONS AND CUSTOMS FROM AROUND THE WORLD

WRITTEN BY

PAMELA KENNEDY

ART RESEARCH BY

F. LYNNE BACHLEDA

IDEALS CHILDREN'S BOOKS • NASHVILLE, TENNESSEE

For Annie, who makes each day a celebration.

- P. K.

Published by Ideals Publishing Corporation
Nashville, Tennessee 37210

Printed and bound in the United States of America

Library of Congress Cataloging-in-Publication Data

Kennedy, Pamela, 1946-
    An Easter Celebration: traditions and customs from around the world / by Pamela Kennedy; photo research by F. Lynne Bachleda.
        p.   cm.
    Summary: Examines the history, symbols, and customs of Easter and Holy Week around the world.
    ISBN 0-8249-8506-0
    1. Easter—Juvenile literature. 2. Holy Week—Juvenile literature. [1. Easter. 2. Holy Week.] I. Bachleda, F. Lynne. II. Title.
GT4935.K46   1991
394.2'68283—dc20   90-21722
                                                    CIP
                                                    AC

Designed by Patrick T. McRae

The text type is Berkeley.
The display type is Shelley Allegro.
Color separations made by Rayson Films, Inc., Waukesha, Wisconsin.
Printed and bound by Worzalla Publishing Company, Stevens Point, Wisconsin.

Art credits:

Cover *Easter Window,* St. Matthew Lutheran Church, St. Paul, Minnesota; Robert Berg. The Crosiers/Gene Plaisted. **3** *On the Road to Emmaus;* Ideals Art Archives. **4-5** *Easter,* Elim Lutheran Church, Robbinsdale, Minnesota; The Crosiers/Gene Plaisted. **6** *Spring Flowers;* John Netherton. **7** detail of *La Primavera;* Botticelli. Firenze Gall. degli Uffizi. Scala/Art Resource, N.Y. **10** (left) *Fabergé silver-gilt and shaded Easter Egg;* by Fedor Ruckert, Moscow, ca. 1900. *Fabergé silver-gilt and shaded enamel Kovsh;* Moscow, 1908-17. *Fabergé silver-gilt and shaded enamel jeweled Easter Egg,* by Fedor Ruckert, Moscow, ca. 1900. Art Resource, N.Y. (right) *Rose Trellis Egg;* Walters Art Gallery/Baltimore. **11** *Decorated Eggs Still Life;* Rick Rusing/Tony Stone Worldwide/Chicago, Ltd. **12** *Buying Easter Flowers;* W.P. Snyder, North Wind Picture Archives. **13** *Christ's Entry into Jerusalem;* North Wind Picture Archives. **14** (top) *An Easter Postcard,* ca. 1909; Culver Pictures. (bottom) *Brown Hare;* Albrecht Dürer, 1509. Culver Pictures. **15** (left) *The First Passover;* North Wind Picture Archives. (right) *Jesus;* North Wind Picture Archives. **16** *Buying Easter Bonnets;* W.A. Rogers, ca. 1890, North Wind Picture Archives. **17** *Maestà;* Duccio, retro, part; lavanda dei piedi. Siena, Opera del Duomo. Scala/Art Resource, N.Y. **19** *Boys Cracking Eggs;* E.A. Abbey, ca. 1870, North Wind Picture Archives. **20-21** *Ash Wednesday,* St. Stephen Anoka Church; The Crosiers/Gene Plaisted. **22** *La Maestà;* Duccio, retro. L'Ultima Cena. Siena, Museo dell'Opera Metropolitana. Scala/Art Resource, N.Y. **23** *The Last Supper;* John Baker, ca. 1835, Culver Pictures. **25** *Salita al Calvario;* Tintoretto. Venezia, S. Rocco. Scala/Art Resource, N.Y. **26** *"Hot Cross Buns!"* ca. 1861. North Wind Picture Archives. **27** *Hot Cross Buns;* Anthony Blake Photo Library/Gerrit Buntrock. **28** *Transfiguration;* Raphael. Vaticano, Pinacoteca-Pittura, Scala/Art Resource, N.Y. **30-31** *Dogwood;* John Netherton. **31** and **backcover** *Lilies;* The Crosiers/Gene Plaisted.

CONTENTS

On the first day of the week, very early in the morning, the women took the spices they had prepared and went to the tomb. They found the stone rolled away from the tomb, but when they entered, they did not find the body of the Lord Jesus. While they were wondering about this, suddenly two men in clothes that gleamed like lightning stood beside them.

In their fright the women bowed down with their faces to the ground, but the men said to them, "Why do you look for the living among the dead? He is not here; he has risen!"

Luke 24:1-6a

This story of the very first Easter is as clear and simple today as it was two thousand years ago. Since then, however, Easter has become the most important holiday in Christianity, embracing not just a single day, but an entire season of celebration.

The Easter season overflows with special days like Palm Sunday and Good Friday, important symbols like the cross and the candle, and interesting customs like sunrise services and parades.

Many of Easter's customs began long before the time of Christ. As people all over the world accepted Christianity, they gave these traditions new meanings connected to their faith in Christ and to their belief in his Resurrection.

5

*L*ong before Jesus walked on the earth, people celebrated when spring arrived. Many of Easter's interesting and often unusual customs began hundreds, even thousands of years ago during the spring!

In ancient times, people did not know why the seasons changed. They thought the times of the seasons were guided by spirits or gods and goddesses. Some even thought the sun died when winter came!

When spring arrived, they were happy to see plants blooming, animals coming out of hibernation, and birds returning from far away. These ancient people expressed their joy in the arrival of spring with many different celebrations.

The Celts lived in what is now the greater part of western Europe, mainly from 2000 B.C. to 100 B.C. Their religion was called Druidism, and they believed in good and evil spirits. These prehistoric people thought that winter came when evil spirits captured the sun god. When spring began each year, the Celts lit huge bonfires, hoping to frighten the evil spirits into releasing the sun.

In some countries today, such as Germany and Belgium, bonfires are still a part of Easter celebrations. The use of a large candle in Easter services today is also traced to these ancient customs.

The ancient Greeks believed that gods and goddesses were in charge of the earth. A Greek story says the goddess Demeter's daughter was kidnapped while picking flowers and afterward was allowed to visit her mother only during the spring and summer. When each spring arrived, the Greeks believed Demeter's happiness made the flowers bloom. They thought her sadness caused winter to return when her daughter went away again.

The daughter was said to have been picking narcissus when she was captured, so it became a flower of special meaning to the Greeks. In many parts of the world, the narcissus, with its bright and fragrant blossoms, has long been a favorite Easter flower.

In ancient Rome, people also thought that a goddess made the flowers bloom. They called her Flora and held the Festival of Floralia to honor her each spring. During this time, Romans held big parades and carried garlands of blossoms through the streets where statues of Flora were lavishly decorated with flowers.

*I*n ancient Egypt, the Hebrews were kept as slaves, so God sent Moses to free them. When the ruler, Pharoah, would not let the Hebrews go, God punished Egypt in many ways. He finally sent the Angel of Death to destroy the firstborn in each family—but first He told the Hebrews to make a special lamb offering, and the angel would *pass over* their homes.

This first Passover is commemorated each year by members of the Jewish faith, about March 21. For many years, Easter was celebrated at this same time because Jesus was crucified during Passover.

In A.D. 325, a group of men meeting in Nicaea, a city in what we now call Turkey, decided that Easter should be on a different day.

They chose the Sunday following the first full moon after the vernal equinox. Vernal means "spring," and equinox means "equal night." Thus, this is the one 24-hour period in the spring when both day and night last exactly twelve hours, usually on March 21 or 22.

Full moons, however, do not always come on the same date, so Easter may fall on any Sunday between March 22 and April 25. Sometimes it comes *before* Passover, and many Orthodox or Eastern Christians wait until Passover to celebrate Easter.

*E*arly Christians called Easter *Pesach*, which is the Hebrew name for Passover. Today, names for Easter all over the world are similar to the word *Pesach*. In France, Easter is called *Pâques*; in Spain, it is *Pascua*; and in Italy, *Pasqua*. The Norwegians call Easter *Paaske*, the Dutch call it *Paach*, and the Swedish call it *Pask*. In Albania, Easter is *Pashkë*; and in Greece, Easter is *Pascha*.

Our English name "Easter" is newer than other European names for the holiday. Before Christianity was accepted in early England, the people there celebrated each vernal equinox with a feast honoring their goddess of the spring who was named Eostre.

About 1,400 years ago, the early English Christians wanted others to accept Christianity, so they decided to use the name Easter for their holiday so that it would match the name of the old spring celebration.

Early Christians often embraced the names and customs of ancient holidays so that it would be more comfortable for other people to accept and believe in Christianity.

9

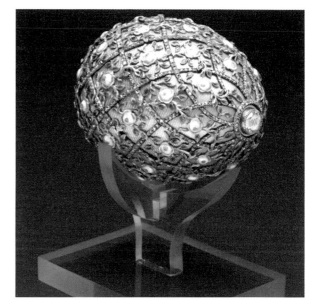

$\mathcal{A}$s Christians traveled and shared Christ's story, more and more people came to believe in him. They began to see their familiar traditions, symbols, and celebrations of spring in a new way. These old traditions became more than a celebration of spring, and were seen as beautiful symbols of Christ defeating death and coming back to life.

The egg is one of the oldest spring symbols in the world. Primitive people knew that the oval shape of the egg was the same shape of both a raindrop and a seed, two important life-giving elements. They saw the egg as a promise of new life. In the spring, when birds and reptiles hatched from eggs, people knew that life would continue, and so they celebrated.

Ancient Persians, Phoenicians, Hindus, and Egyptians all believed that the world began with a single egg. One legend tells of a great egg which broke in half. One half of the shell formed the earth, one half became the sky, and the yolk became the sun!

Eggs were given as springtime gifts in ancient China, Greece, and Rome. As the story of Christ's Resurrection spread over the world, people saw the egg as a symbol of the stone tomb from which Christ rose. They viewed the hatching birds and chicks as symbols of the new life Jesus promised his followers. Even though they had given eggs as gifts in the past, the gift of an egg now had a newer, deeper meaning.

In England, in the Middle Ages, members of royal families gave one another gold-covered eggs as Easter gifts. Even though most people could not afford eggs of gold, they still enjoyed decorating eggs. Sometimes they wrapped leaves, flowers, or ferns around an egg before boiling it and the plants' patterns would be printed on the egg.

In Russia and Poland, women and girls spent hours drawing intricate designs on Easter eggs. In early America, children colored eggs using dyes made from bark, berries, and leaves.

From 1870 until 1918, Peter Fabergé was the most famous Easter egg decorator. He designed eggs from gold, silver, and precious gems for the kings of Europe and czars of Russia. Each egg cost thousands of dollars. Fabergé eggs are now priceless works of art which may be found only in museums and private collections.

Egg decorating is still practiced by artists who design beautiful eggs which open to reveal tiny scenes, music boxes, or even moving toys!

*I*n ancient times, huge bonfires were lit in the spring. When people became Christians, their spring fires represented the light coming to the world through Christ. Early Christians often lit bonfires on the night before Easter.

Now the candle is used as a symbol of the light of Christ. Many churches use a large, white Paschal candle in their Easter decorations.

On Easter Eve, in the Greek Orthodox church, congregation members line up outside the front door holding lighted candles. One person knocks at the door and asks, "Is Jesus inside?" Someone within calls, "No, he is not here. He is risen!" Then the door is opened wide and the people enter their church in glowing candlelight.

Long ago, people put out all of the fires in their homes on Easter Eve. On Easter morning, "new fire" was taken from the one large Easter candle at church as a sign of the new life offered by Christ.

Before the time of Christ, the cross was also a well-known symbol, used as a special mark on clothes and buildings. In Jesus' time, the cross was a sign of death, because Romans used crosses to punish criminals. When Jesus was crucified, believers saw the cross as a symbol of his suffering. Soon after the Resurrection, however, Christians began to see the cross as a sign of Jesus' victory over death.

Today, Easter cakes, breads, flower arrangements, and cards are made in the shape of the cross. On Good Friday, buns decorated with white frosting crosses are enjoyed as breakfast treats. For the Christian, the cross is a symbol of hope. And around the world, the cross is recognized as the mark of those who follow Christ.

12

*D*uring Christ's time, it was a Roman custom to welcome royalty by waving palm branches. When Jesus entered Jerusalem on the first Palm Sunday, people cut branches from palm trees, blanketed the streets with them, and waved them in the air shouting "Hosanna! Blessed is he who comes in the name of the Lord!"

Today, on Palm Sunday, Christians all over the world carry palm branches in parades, make palm strips into crosses, and weave palm leaves into garlands for church decorations. In countries where palms do not grow, other plants are used instead.

Another favorite Eastertime plant is the lily. The Easter lily is new in the celebration of Easter, first brought to the United States in 1882 from Bermuda. On Easter morning, churches fill their altars with these lovely, waxy white flowers as a reminder of Christ's purity.

The Easter Bunny is a popular part of many Easter celebrations in the United States, but its story goes back thousands of years.

In Egypt long ago, people believed the rabbit was responsible for the new life that abounded in the spring. Later, early Christians saw the connection between the rabbit and new life as a symbol for the Resurrection as well.

An old European legend says that the hare, a relative of the rabbit, never closed its eyes. Since it watched the other animals all night long, the hare became a symbol of the moon. The hare was soon connected with Easter because the holiday's date depends upon the full moon.

An old German story tells of a poor woman who loved children and enjoyed giving them Easter treats. One year, she hid brightly colored eggs in her garden, and while the children searched for them, they saw a hare hopping past. They thought the hare had left the eggs!

German children made nests of leaves and branches in their gardens for the "Easter Hare." Some children left nests made of clothes or a hat in quiet corners of their homes. When German children came to the United States, they brought this custom with them.

Rabbits were more common in the United States than were hares, so the Easter Hare became the Easter Rabbit, and later, it was called the Easter Bunny. Early American children built nests of leaves and sticks in their gardens or barns for the Easter Rabbit to fill with colored eggs. Today, the Easter Bunny often brings his own baskets!

14

*L*ong before the first Passover, Hebrew families gave lambs as offerings to God. And since the first Passover, Hebrews serve lamb as an important part of the Passover feast each year.

When Jesus died during Passover, he gave himself as an offering to God for the sins of all the world. This is why the Bible calls Jesus the Lamb of God. Early Christians saw the lamb as a beautiful symbol of Jesus and began using it in their Easter celebrations.

Banners and flags decorated with pictures of lambs were carried in Easter celebrations during the Middle Ages. Later, in England, small Easter "pax cakes" were made with the imprint of a lamb on top.

Easter celebrations in many countries now feature candies and pastries shaped like lambs. A beautifully decorated Easter lamb cake is often the centerpiece of Easter tables in European countries.

15

Early Christians living in the first hundred years after the Resurrection called the week before Easter "White Week." They believed that this was an especially good time to be baptized and they wore new, white clothes as a sign of their new life.

Two hundred years later, the emperor Constantine, too, saw clothing as a way to express a new life in Christ. In honor of the Resurrection, he ordered his council to dress up in their most elegant robes and march through the streets of Rome on Easter.

Later in European countries, people came to believe that a new piece of clothing worn on Easter Sunday would bring good luck all year long. As people walked to and from church in their new clothes, they visited and admired one another. Soon this simple Easter walk became a parade, an event which everyone looked forward to all during the cold, dark winter months.

One of the most famous Easter parades today takes place along Fifth Avenue in New York City. It began as a casual stroll home from church, but in the early 1900s, it became a great fashion parade. Fancy hats decorated with flowers, ribbons, and even birds in nests are especially popular in New York's Easter parade.

*F*oot washing is one of the lesser-known customs of the Easter season, but perhaps is one of the most important. At the time of Christ, people wore sandals and walked many miles on dusty roads. It was a sign of courtesy and respect for a servant to gently wash the feet of guests when they arrived.

The night before he was crucified, Jesus took a basin of water and a towel, and washed the feet of each of his disciples. Christ was showing his followers that he was their servant, and that he respected them. Christ knew he was leaving the disciples to start his church, and he was also showing them that in order to be good leaders, they must both show respect to their followers and also be willing to serve them.

In medieval times, kings and lords followed Christ's example by washing the feet of twelve of the poorest men in their kingdoms on the Thursday before Easter. Later, in England, it became the custom of the kings and queens to wash the feet of as many poor people as they were years old. Queen Elizabeth still carries on this custom today.

*M*aking an Easter tree is an old custom in Holland, Germany, France, and Switzerland. In the days before Easter, bare branches are brought into European houses and mounted in pots filled with earth.

Children busily hollow out eggshells by poking small holes in the ends of their eggs and draining the liquid. They use ribbons and dyes to decorate their eggs, and then hang them on the bare branches.

The decorated Easter tree reminds a family of Christ's Resurrection from death because the eggs are a symbol of life adorning the dry branches which symbolize death. German and Dutch families brought the custom of the Easter tree to the United States.

Games involving eggs have long been enjoyed in many parts of the world at Eastertime. In England, eggs are placed along a racetrack and children race to gather the most eggs in a set length of time. This game is also played in Germany's Black Forest, but there, the contestants ride on horseback or on bicycles!

Egg breaking games have been popular for centuries in many different countries, too. In England it is called Egg Picking, or Egg Shakling, and children hold hard-boiled eggs in their hands and knock them lightly against the eggs held by others. When players' eggs break, they must give them to their opponents. The champion is the child whose egg has the hardest shell!

Easter egg hunts are customary all over the world. Held on or near Easter Sunday, egg hunts often have separate areas for younger and older children, and the winner is the child who finds the most eggs.

Egg rolling was started in Europe hundreds of years ago. Gathering on gentle slopes or hillsides, contestants rolled their eggs toward the finish line at the bottom of the hill. The first unbroken egg over the finish line was the winning entry.

In the United States, an annual egg roll was started during the presidency of James Madison over 180 years ago. The White House south lawn became the site of the Easter Monday Egg Roll, and hundreds of children participate in this traditional event. Adults are not allowed to roll eggs, and the only adults allowed to watch the game are those accompanied by children!

The Christian celebration of Easter is really a season of special days pointing to the death and Resurrection of Jesus Christ. As people from many lands became believers in Christ, they each added unique touches to this season called Lent.

Lent is a period of fasting, or doing without certain foods. Not counting Sundays, Lent is the forty days before Easter. Many Christians fast during this time to remind themselves of the forty days Jesus fasted in the wilderness.

Several countries have celebrations just before Lent begins. In England, Shrove Tuesday is the name given to the last day before Lent. On this day, many people make pancakes in order to use up all their eggs, butter, and milk before it is time to fast.

In other countries, the last few days before Lent are filled with parties, masquerade balls, parades, festivals, and in some places, fireworks displays. This period of celebration is often called Carnival. In Europe, Carnival is held in Norway, Switzerland, France, Italy, Spain, Germany, Portugal, and Greece. Carnival is also held in almost all of the countries in Central and South America, as well as in the islands of the Caribbean and in Cuba.

In the United States, Carnival is held in very few places; among those the most famous is in New Orleans, Louisiana. The French settled New Orleans, and in their language, Mardi Gras means "Fat Tuesday." Their Carnival begins six days before Lent and ends with a Mardi Gras festival involving tens of thousands of people and a parade of colorful floats, bands, and marching units.

Ash Wednesday is the first day of Lent. On this day, many Christian churches have a special service of prayer, during which the priest or minister may sprinkle ashes upon the heads of the people or make a small cross of ashes on the forehead of each worshipper.

On Ash Wednesday in many countries, people make and eat pretzels. The word pretzel comes from a Latin word meaning "little arms." The shape of the twisted pretzel is meant to remind people of arms folded in prayer. Pretzels are easy and fun to make!

HOW TO MAKE PRETZELS

²/₃ cups warm water	¹/₄ cup shortening
1 pkg. dry yeast	2 cups flour
1 tsp. salt	1 egg white
1 tbsp. sugar	coarse salt

Put water in a bowl and add yeast. Stir until yeast is dissolved. Add all other ingredients except coarse salt; stir until mixed well. Place dough on a floured board and knead about 6-8 minutes until dough is smooth. Cover and let dough rise in a warm place for about an hour or until doubled. Punch down dough and let it rest about 10 minutes.

Roll golf ball sized pieces of dough into strips about as thick as a pencil. Twist the strips into pretzel shapes and place on a lightly greased cookie sheet. Brush tops with egg white mixed with a little water, then sprinkle coarse salt on the pretzels. Let pretzels rise for about 30 minutes, then bake for 15 minutes in a 400° oven.

*P*alm Sunday marks the beginning of Holy Week. On this day, early Christians carried palm branches to church remembering how Jesus was welcomed to Jerusalem on the first Palm Sunday.

Since medieval times, palm leaves have been twisted into cross shapes and given to Christian worshipers on Palm Sunday. On the Ash Wednesday of the following year, these shapes are brought back to church, burned to ash, and used by priests during church services. Palm leaves are also used in Jewish services during Passover.

The Latin American countries often have huge parades on Palm Sunday, featuring tall statues of Jesus and Mary which are sometimes so heavy that it takes dozens of men to carry each one!

In many countries, palm branches are used to decorate churches. In countries where palms are not available, willow, myrtle, bay, pussywillow, olive, or boxwood branches are used instead.

Children in Austria hang pretzels on their palm branches. And in Finland, children used to cut willow branches early on Palm Sunday and lightly switch the women in their neighborhood for good luck!

HOW TO MAKE A PALM BRANCH

It is easy to make a replica of a palm branch from a piece of construction paper. First, fold a piece of green construction paper in half, lengthwise. Now cut a long, narrow semi-oval from one end of the paper to the other. Keeping paper folded, cut in narrow lines toward, but not through, the fold. Open your palm branch!

The Thursday before Easter is called Maundy Thursday. The name Maundy comes from a Latin word which means command. It refers to the new commandment Jesus gave his disciples on the Thursday before he was crucified. On that night long ago, he served their Last Supper of bread and wine, washed his disciples' feet, and said, "A new command I give you: Love one another. As I have loved you, so you must love one another." John 13:34

As a reminder of these things, Christians often re-enact the acts of foot washing and serving communion on Maundy Thursday.

During the Middle Ages, people rang church bells all during Maundy Thursday services, and then silenced the bells until Easter Eve. Spring cleaning, a custom associated with the return of warmer weather, pre-dates Christ, but is another tradition adopted by Christians and practiced on Maundy Thursday. In preparation for Easter Sunday, people of long ago spent this day washing and sweeping their homes and carefully cleaning their bodies as well.

Another interesting custom traced to the Middle Ages is the wearing of green and eating of only green foods on this day. For this reason, it is still called "Green Thursday" in many parts of Europe, and salads and greens are a favorite menu. In Austria, people use and eat only green eggs on this day!

*G*ood Friday used to be called God's Friday because it was the day Jesus was crucified. This is the most solemn day of the year for Christians as they recall the suffering and death of Jesus.

In past times, there were many superstitions connected with Good Friday. Miners were afraid to go down into the mines because they thought the earth was cursed on that day when Jesus was laid in the tomb. Blacksmiths refused to pound a nail because nails were used in the crucifixion. And many housewives thought it was bad luck to wash clothes on Good Friday because Christ had been wrapped in linen cloths on this day.

Farmers, however, believed seeds planted on Good Friday would yield wonderful crops. Some people collected water in containers on this day because they thought it could cure eye diseases!

The Bible says that when Jesus hung on the cross, the sky became dark from noon until three o'clock in the afternoon. Long ago, Christians held quiet church services during these three hours on Good Friday. Statues and pictures of Christ were draped in black cloth and prayers were offered for forgiveness of sins.

The special devotion called the "Stations of the Cross" was started during the Crusades six hundred years ago. Pictures or statues were placed along a city street. Each one was called a "station" and showed a different part of Christ's trial, death, or burial. Christians walked from station to station, reciting prayers at each one.

Today many Protestant and Catholic churches hold Good Friday services from noon until three, and almost all Catholic churches are decorated with pictures or statues depicting the stations of the Cross.

*L*ong before Jesus' time, the Celts made and ate sweet cakes or rolls to enjoy at their springtime celebrations. With the spread of Christianity, many people no longer believed in the old gods of the sun and the seasons, but they still loved to eat their delicate sweet breads in the spring.

Since long ago, people in Great Britain have enjoyed the traditional Good Friday breakfast of hot cross buns. They are marked with a white icing cross to remind people of Christ. When street vendors sold their wares in London, they sang a song that has become a favorite nursery rhyme for children:

Hot cross buns! Hot cross buns!
One a penny, two a penny, hot cross buns!
If you have no daughters, give them to your sons,
One a penny, two a penny, hot cross buns!

26

HOW TO MAKE HOT CROSS BUNS

1 cup milk, scalded

1/2 cup sugar

3 tbsp. melted butter

1/2 tsp. salt

1 pkg. dry yeast

1/4 cup warm water

1 egg, well beaten

3 cups flour

1 tsp. cinnamon

1/2 cup raisins

1 tsp. grated orange peel

1 cup powdered sugar

2 tsp. milk

Mix together milk, sugar, butter, and salt. Let cool. Dissolve yeast in warm water. Add dissolved yeast and egg and mix well. Stir flour and cinnamon into mixture then add raisins and orange peel and mix well.

Cover bowl with a cloth and place in a warm spot until dough is double—about 1-1½ hours.

Shape dough into round buns and place all except one on a lightly greased cookie sheet. Cover buns on sheet and let rise for one hour.

While buns are rising, use a rolling pin to roll the extra bun ¼ inch thick on a floured surface. Cut into strips ¼ inch wide, and set aside.

Make a cross on each bun with a sharp knife. Gently press a strip of dough into each cut and pinch off the ends at the base of buns.

Bake in the oven at 400° for 20 minutes.

While buns are baking, mix powdered sugar and milk together.

When buns are baked, remove from oven and let cool slightly. Then drizzle icing across the top of each bun.

$\mathcal{E}$aster Eve is a time of interesting extremes. In many European countries, people have solemn candlelight services. In other countries, such as Italy and Spain, and those in Latin America, the day is filled with the noise of bands playing and people singing. As the sun sets and the sky darkens, huge firework displays explode, cannons fire, bells ring, and whistles blow. The noisy celebrations express the joy people feel as they anticipate Jesus' Resurrection.

In countries of Northern Europe, such as Norway and Sweden, huge bonfires blaze in the Easter Eve darkness. It is said that fires were lit in the spring thousands of years ago by people who thought they could help heat up the earth after the long, cold winter. Now, however, these fires symbolize the coming of Christ, and often burn until the sun comes up on Easter morning.

For many, Easter Sunday begins in the pre-dawn darkness as they wait for the first rays of sun to lighten the Eastern sky. In ancient times, the sun was worshiped as the giver of life, and when the darkness of winter ended, many people believed that the sun danced in the sky. For this reason, they gathered on hilltops to watch the sun rise on the first day of spring each year.

As Christianity spread throughout the world, people saw Christ as the giver of life and turned from worshiping the sun to honoring him. As they recalled the story of the women coming to Christ's empty tomb at dawn, believers thought of the sunrise on Easter as a symbol of the Resurrection.

*E*aster Sunday is the most joyful of all Christian celebrations. All over the world, Christians gather at dawn to greet the rising sun with the victorious cry, "Christ is risen!" Long ago in France, people gathered outside to watch for the first sunbeams of Easter, believing that they were God's angels dancing for joy.

An old Irish custom was to hold a dance contest as the sun rose on Easter morning. The men danced and women baked a cake to be used as a prize for the winner. It is thought that the expression "he takes the cake" comes from this old Irish tradition.

In early America, Easter services were very simple, reflecting the Puritan or Quaker heritage of many of the early settlers. Today, however, Easter services are elaborate and often feature huge choirs and even pageants or plays depicting parts of the Easter story.

One of the largest Easter services is in Rome at St. Peter's Square. Thousands of people gather from all over the world to hear the Easter message given by the Pope, the leader of the Catholic church.

On Easter morning, churches everywhere are decorated with beautiful flowers and their choirs sing great cantatas like Handel's Messiah. People wear their new clothes for Easter Sunday services in honor of the new life they have in Christ.

Churches are often completely full as members come together to rejoice and to offer praise to God. The sadness of Good Friday disappears as people remember the Resurrection of Jesus Christ and his promise of eternal life.

*T*here are many beautiful Easter legends about the flowers which bloom in the spring. As people looked at these flowers and thought about Easter, they made up stories to explain how the blossoms related to the death of Jesus. Two of these legends are about the dogwood and the lily.

THE LEGEND OF THE DOGWOOD

*L*ong, long ago, when Jesus walked upon the earth, the dogwood tree was tall and proud. Its trunk was as large around as an oak tree and its wood was hard and strong. Near the city of Jerusalem grew an especially lovely dogwood tree.

When Jesus was to be crucified, the Roman soldiers looked at the tree and decided it would be just the right kind of wood for a cross. They cut down the tree and made a cross for Jesus.

But the dogwood tree was very sad and ashamed to be put to such a terrible use. Jesus knew the tree was very unhappy and he felt sorry for it. He promised the dogwood that it would never again grow large enough to be used as a cross. And then, to give the world a reminder of the tree's history, Jesus gave it a very special blossom. This blossom would be a sign of Jesus' death.

That is why the dogwood's four white petals form the shape of a cross. On the outer edge of each petal there is a dark red stain, as a reminder that Jesus was offered on the cross for forgiveness of sins. And in the center of each bloom is a tiny crown of thorns.

THE LEGEND OF THE EASTER LILY

*I*n the Garden of Gethsemane, there were many beautiful flowers, but the loveliest of all was the pure white lily. The lily knew it was very beautiful, and it proudly lifted its head to show itself to anyone who happened to pass by the garden.

On the night before he was crucified, Jesus came into the quiet Garden of Gethsemane to pray. As he prayed and wept there, the flowers of the garden bowed their heads in pity and sorrow too. But the proud lily would not bow its lovely white head.

The next day, the lily discovered that Jesus was going to be crucified. The flower felt so miserable about how it had acted in the garden that it bowed its head in shame. To honor the Lord Jesus and to show its sorrow, the lily has grown with a down-turned blossom ever since that first Good Friday of long, long ago.

31

$\mathcal{A}$ll the traditions of Easter, from the eggs and rabbits to the hymns and legends, blend together to make this wonderful holiday a time of joy and celebration.

We celebrate Easter with singing and praises to God because we remember that Jesus Christ is alive. He lives today to give each person new life and hope. This is the truth of Easter.